1

BROKEN, BUT NOT DESTROYED

VELMA "ANGELICA" ATKINS

Dedication

I would like to dedicate this book to my husband, children,

grandchildren and my mother for their love, support and

dedication.   I would also like to dedicate this book to those who

lives have been impacted by any form of abuse.

Table of Contents

Chapter 1

The Beginning of Struggles

Proverbs 4:1-2- Hear, ye children, the instruction of a father, and
attend to know understanding. For I give you good doctrine,
forsake ye not my law.

I have never known life without struggles. In fact, my struggles

began the day I was born. According to my mother, the day she

went into labor with me was dark and gloomy. She was at home

alone working around the house while my dad was at work. As

she did her housework she went into labor. Being very young she

had no idea what to do. Long story short, I was born at home

without the aid of a doctor or mid-wife. I don't know all of the

details, but I do know that it was not until my mother's aunt

Gloria came by later that I was taken to see a doctor.

Gloria took us both to the local clinic so that the doctors could

make sure that everything was ok. After the doctor had examined

both my mother and me, we were discharged home.

It wasn't long after we were discharged from the clinic that my dad came home from work. Shocked to see a baby in the bed, especially one with light skin and light colored eyes; he begins to question my mom. Apparently, he did not believe that I was his child, because he did not see any of his attributes and features. My mother reassured him that she had been faithful to him and that I was his child? I am told he was still not convinced and he could be heard praying and asking God to give him the courage to love me, in the event that I was not his child.

My mother felt as if she was in a difficult position. She knew I was his child, but she needed him to know it as well. They were not doing DNA test the way they are now, so the only thing she could do was pray that God would show him that I was indeed his child. Later that night, she begins to see some sign that her prayer just might be working. As I lay in the bed crying, my dad came in to attend to my needs. She stood at the door and watched him as he rocked me in his arms and called me a gift from God. This gave my mother a great sense of peace and brought a level of calmness to her. She didn't know how long it would take for him to be convinced, but she knew that God was in control and that everything happens for a reason. She knew that all she had to do was have faith and believe that God would turn things around.

Chapter 2

A Twist of Faith

Deuteronomy 8:11- Beware that thou forget not the LORD thy

God, in not keeping his commandments, and his judgments, and

his statutes, which I command thee this day:

My mom had a sister name Anna. Anna was very protective of me,

especially since she did not have any children of her own at the

time. She would often stop by, pick me up and take me home with

her. This would give my parents time to relax and do other

things. My mother would use the time to cook, clean and get

things ready for my father to come home from work.

After one particular visit from my aunt, my mom put me to bed

and fixed dinner for my dad. Not realizing that my dad had gotten

off work earlier in the day and had spent the afternoon drinking

with his friends. He was intoxicated and he began verbally

abusing my mother. He called her everything but a child of God

and once again begin accusing her of being unfaithful. He told her

that I was not his baby and that my father had to be a white man.

My mother denied ever being with another man during the course of their marriage, but my father refused to believe her. He replied, "That baby's skin is too light, and nobody in my family has eyes that change colors like that!" He yelled and screamed so loudly that it finally awakens me out of my sleep and I begin to cry. My mother rushes to try to calm me, but before she can make it to my side my dad knocks her to the floor with his fist. He doesn't stop there. Once she is down he continue to beat her with his fist. She tries her best to get away and even attempts to fight back, but he is just too strong. When she is finally able to get away, she picks me up and notices that my body is hot and that I am burning up with fever.

She tells my father that I am burning up with fever. However, he is so intoxicated and filled with rage that he does not seem to care at all. My mother hopes and prays that the fever is simply due to teething, but when I begin to shake, she knows it's more serious. She begged and pleaded with my father to take me to the hospital so that she could see what was wrong with me. He finally sobered up enough to drive and agreed to take us.

11

When we pulled up to the hospital, my father who was now sober could see the bruises and the beating that he put on my mother. Before he would let her go into the hospital, he apologized. My mother accepted his apology of course. Her main focus was to make sure that her child was ok. Once inside the hospital, I was rushed to the back to be seen by hospital staff. Even though they were taking care of me, they also noticed the bruises on my mother. They begin to question her about our home environment. My mother covered for my father's alcoholism and abuse.

I was admitted to the hospital that night. My mother stayed with me but my dad returned home. I am told that my dad once again fell down on his knees and prayed for God. This time he prayed that God would forgive him for doubting that I was his child and that God would heal my body. He returned to the hospital early the next morning and found my mother asleep with me in her arms. He leaned over, kissed my forehead and said a prayer of thanks to God for letting me make it through the night. My mother awoke to see who it was that was standing over us. When she did she noticed that he had tears streaming down his face and looked like he had been awake all night. She asked him if he had gotten any sleep and he replied no. He stated that he could not sleep because he was worried about me.

Soon after that, the doctor came in to give them the report of what was wrong with me. He told them that I was not getting the proper nutrition. He said it was a good thing that I got to the hospital when I did or I might have died. My dad begins to pray and thank God again for letting me make it through.

Even though he had his doubts about my paternity, my dad would always pray and ask God for guidance concerning me. I want to stop here and encourage you that no matter what you have done wrong, how low you have fallen; if you seek God he will come to your rescue every time. All you need to do is be sincere and willing to let him be the Lord of your life.

Chapter 3

A New Dawn

Matthew 15:11-Not that which goeth into the mouth that defileth a man; but that which cometh out of the mouth, this defileth a man.

Psalm 30:5- For his anger *endureth* but a moment; in his favor *is* life: weeping may endure for a night but joy *cometh* in the morning.

Time passed and I was now a toddler. It wasn't long and my mother was pregnant again. My mother had her hands full being pregnant with an active toddler as well as having to take care of my dad. She said I was a busy body and that I got into everything. So you can imagine her delight when her cousin Gwen came by and asked if she wanted her to take me home with her for a little while so that she could get some rest.

It wasn't long before my mother gave birth to my younger sister. I was so excited to be a big sister. It was like having a real life doll. I now had somebody to play with. I was so very protective over her. Especially since the arguments and fights between my mother and father seemed to get worst.

One day after a big fight between my mother and father my sister and I were left alone in the living room while our parents were in their bedroom. My sister began to cry; even though I was not much older than her I tried to care for her. I gave her a pacifier but she still did not stop crying. So I picked her up and tried to take her to our parents but on the way I accidently dropped her on a hot heater. My sister let out a scream that scared me, and caused my parents to run out of their room. I was trying to pick her up off the heater when my mother ran in and snatched her from me. She yells, screams and even gets a switch and gave me a terrible whooping. This made me afraid to get close to my sister. I was scared that I would make a mistake again and get a whooping for it. I never felt loved by either of my parents. I felt as if I could not do anything right. I was an outcast. So I began to withdraw, and pretend that I did not even exist.

I would get whipped for any and everything. I remember one day in particular when my parents were fighting. My dad had taken a cigarette lighter and was threatening to set my mother on fire by her hair and burn her up. I was crying, pulling on his leg and begging him not to hurt or kill my mother. I will never forget that moment as long as I live. Not only because of what he threatened to do to my mother, but because of what he did to me. My dad took a belt, put it around my neck and threatened to kill me. My mother begged and pleaded with my dad to let me go. I was gasping for air trying to catch my breath when he finally let me go. Unfortunately, it wasn't over. My mother then took the belt that my dad had around my neck and begin to beat me with it, saying that I should never have come in the room where they were arguing.

The fights didn't stop there. My dad was always coming home drunk and beating on my mom. When he got tired of beating on her, he would turn his anger towards me. To make matters worst my mother begin to blame me for him beating on her. She once told me that if I had never been born or if I had died when I was sick, she would not be going through his abuse. How could a mother blame a little child for such a grown up situation? I never asked to be born. I didn't do anything to make him hit her. I was so hurt and confused. What did I do to deserve this type of treatment? When will things get better for me? I did not feel loved or wanted by my parents, so even as a little child, I begin battling depression.

The fights between my parents never stopped. Unfortunately, in between the arguments and fights the babies kept coming. My mom had one daughter that died at birth of an unknown sickness. Not long after that another one of my sisters died of Sudden Infant Death Syndrome or what my parents called "Crib death". I saw so many hard times and struggles growing up. But I want to encourage you. You are loved. You are cared for. Even when you don't feel love, know that there is someone praying for you. Regardless of the struggles you face, keep your head up. Never allow depression, rejection or abuse to destroy you. I am a living witness that you can survive it all. So whatever you do, stay strong. You may bend, but don't break. You may be broken, but

17

you are not destroyed! So hold on, don't lose heart things will get better. May the following verses give you both comfort and strength during your time of struggle or affliction.

2 Corinthians 4:16-18 (NIV) Therefore we do not lose heart. Though outwardly we are wasting away, yet inwardly we are being renewed day by day. For our light and momentary troubles are achieving for us an eternal glory that far outweighs them all. So we fix our eyes not on what is seen, but on what is unseen, since what is seen is temporary, but what is unseen is eternal.

Chapter 4

Innocence Taken

Isaiah 19:14- The Lord hath mingled a perverse spirit in the midst thereof: and they have caused Egypt to err in every work thereof, as a drunken man staggereth in his vomit.

It's Sunday and my dad is sitting in his favorite chair reading the newspaper. This was his routine every Sunday that he was off from work. I walked in the room where he was and asked him if I could read the paper with him. He laughed because I was only three years old and he did not believe that I could read. He gave me a part of the newspaper and I begin to read the words that I knew. He continued to laugh saying "you really call yourself reading." I replied "I can read, daddy; God taught me how." My dad seemed shocked. He asked "what do you mean God taught you?" I replied, "He really did daddy, and I can read words out of the bible too." My dad still amazed at the claims I was making picked me up and sat me on his lap so that he could see if the words that I was saying matched the words that were in the paper. He gave me the paper and watched me read the words. He was speechless. He called my mother in the room so that she could witness me reading. When my mother came into the room instead of listening to me read, she immediately made me get down from my dad's lap. I was confused. I didn't understand at the time why she would make me get down from my dad's lap. I thought maybe it was because they had been fighting and she was mad at him.

Her reaction was strange. Why can't a daughter sit in her father's lap? Her reaction seemed even stranger when she starting laughing. She told my dad that he was just as crazy as I was if he thought that I was really reading the newspaper. I remember my feeling being hurt and feeling heartbroken because my mother did not believe that I could do it. I don't know if it was the disappointed look on my face or her attempt to make my dad look stupid, but she decided to let me read to her. To her surprise and dismay, I was actually reading. This is the moment that my mother realized that I was truly a gift from God, sent to her and my father.

As days passed and I got a little older, my mother began allowing me to spend time at my aunt Gloria's house. I loved spending time with Aunt Gloria. She would take me to church and even fishing with her. I always felt loved when I was with her. She never made a difference between me and the other kids. When I was there with her I was surrounded by family. My aunt, grandmother and great grandmother all lived within walking distance.

I begin spending time and interacting with my cousins and siblings without a clue as to how my life was about to change. While outside playing with all the other kids, my favorite uncle called me to come to him. I went, not knowing what was about to happen to me. He took me to my grandmother's house; no one was there but him and me. He started touching me, in inappropriate ways. He pulled my panties down and began to do things to me. I began to cry, but he put his hand over my mouth and told me that I better not say anything. He threatens me to never tell anyone what happened. That day changed my life forever. It was the day that my innocence was taken. I went from being a jolly child to one that was sad and withdrawn.

His abuse did not stop that day. I was a young girl, just starting to develop breast bumps. To make matters worst I had other uncles that would touch me inappropriately as well. I got to the point that I hated to even go around any of my uncles. The only uncle that was not sexually abusing me was verbally abusing me. I felt like no one cared for me. I didn't think that God loved me at all. I had so many questions. Why did God allow me to go through such horrible things? Why didn't anyone know what was going on with me? Did they know, but just didn't care? Why didn't anyone see the signs that I was being sexually abused? Why was I the one that my uncles chose to abuse? Was I the only one being abused? I never told and we didn't talk about it as a family, so I have no idea if anyone else was a victim.

I felt so lost and alone. I didn't feel like there was anyone that I could turn to or trust. The longer the molestation continued the more withdrawn I became. It was hard for me to understand all

of this when I was in the midst of the storm. I just remember
hearing that weeping may endure for a night, but joy cometh in
the morning and that God would always be with me.

I am so glad that I learned that God's thoughts are not like our
thoughts. I had no idea that the things that I suffered as a little
girl would some day be the things that I would use to help other
women. I can't help but to be thankful that God did not allow me
to die in the process. Isaiah 59:19b KJV says, "When the enemy
shall come in like a flood, the Spirit of the Lord shall lift up a
standard against him." I didn't realize it at the time, but God
always lifted up a standard against the enemy! He kept me alive!
He kept my mind! He didn't allow depression to take me out! He
kept me in the midst of it all.

It is so easy for us to blame people for what they have done to us
but we have to remember, when Satan has a hold of a person's
mind and heart there is no telling what they will do. All of us have
done some things that we are not proud of and that we regret.
Just take a look at some of the things that were against the law in

Leviticus 20:10-17. Adultery, homosexuality, incest, bestiality (humans having sex with animals), etc. all were punishable by death. How many of those things have you or someone you know been guilty of? I have made a lot of mistakes, but it's my sincere prayer that I can use everything that I have been through to help others.

Chapter 5

What is Prejudice?

According to an article I read on Simple Psychology, **Prejudice** is an unjustified or incorrect attitude (usually negative) towards an individual based solely on the individual's membership of a social group. For example, a person may hold **prejudiced** views towards a certain race or gender.[1] (McLeod, S. A. (2008).

In spite of my struggles at home, I was always a straight A student. I was a starter on my schools basketball team and I ran on the track team as well. I loved school and always had a lot of friends. Even though I grew up in a predominantly white neighborhood, it wasn't until I was in the 7th grade that I had my first real experience with prejudice. My best friend's name was Gabrielle; we called her Gabby for short. Her brother's name was George. George did not like me and would always call me the "N" word. Gabby would take up for me and they would fight about it.

[1] McLeod, S. A. (2008). Prejudice and discrimination. Retrieved from https://www.simplypsychology.org/prejudice.html

Apparently, George went home and told their father about Gabby fighting him over some little black girl on the bus. Their dad was highly upset so the next day he came to the bus stop. Once everyone was on the bus, he boarded the bus to see who the little black girl was that his son was talking about. Once George pointed me out, their dad called me every foul name he could think of. He made Gabby and George get off the bus, and told the bus driver that they were no longer allowed to ride the bus if he was going to allow monkeys ride his bus. Mr. Griffin the bus driver, asked their dad to refrain from the name-calling. He told him it was his right not to have his children ride the bus, if that was what he wanted. He would make a note of it at the schools office. Their dad continued his tirade, until the bus driver made him get off the bus. I was so afraid that day! I had never experienced anything like that in my entire life.

Growing up in church, I had always been taught that God created us all, made us in His image, and that He loved us all the same. I had never seen someone react so full of rage. It was mind-blowing that he was so angry because my skin was a shade darker

26

than his. Even thought this was a horrible experience. I am thankful that my friend Gabby continued to be my friend in spite of what her dad said. I was also thankful for my bus driver, Mr. Griffin. Once we made it to the school he called me to the side and told me that no matter what I heard that morning, I was beautiful both inside and out. He said, their dad was just showing his ignorance.

This day did not seem to be my day. It didn't get better; it only seemed to get worse. It started in my second period art class. We were assigned to do an art project with leaves. So our teacher took us outside to gather leaves. While we were outside there was a dog that was at the fence barking viciously at me. I didn't know why the dog seemed to be targeting me. But by the time we went out for recess the dog had made it's way into the schoolyard and it was chasing me. When the owner came to get the dog, she informed the teacher that the dog had been trained to chase black people. Later when I made it home from school and begin to tell my parents about what happened, I realized that my dad was prejudice too. He hated white people with a passion and he wanted me to feel the same. I just could not believe it! My aunt Gloria had always taught me to love everybody and to treat everyone the way that I wanted to be treated.

The bible says that we were all created from the dust of the ground. No man, woman, boy or girl is better than another. Therefore, to treat someone differently simply because they have a different skin color than you do is just plain ignorant. **1 Corinthians 12:13 (NIV)** says, For we were all baptized by one Spirit so as to form one body—whether Jews or Gentiles, slave or free—and we were all given the one Spirit to drink. **Matthew 22:39 (NIV)**- And the second is like it: 'Love your neighbor as yourself.

The events of that day had me so confused. There were so many negative thoughts running through my mind. I could not understand for the life of me, how people could be so judgmental. I was especially taken aback by my dad's prejudice. I didn't see color; I had friends of all races. I even had family members that were mixed with other races and I thought they were beautiful.

The events of that day, along with the other issues I had faced in my life made me feel ugly both inside and out. I felt so unworthy! I begin to see jealousy stir up in me against my mixed race family members. They had the best of both worlds, they were beautiful and they we partly Mexican. I knew that jealousy was wrong. I had heard sermons over and over again about how pride and jealousy had gotten Lucifer kicked out of Heaven. But I couldn't shake the way that I was feeling.

I felt like I didn't belong in my family. I felt isolated and alone. I had no one that I could share my feeling with. I couldn't talk to my dad because he was always drunk. I tried talking to my mother, but she laughed and sent me to my room, saying that everything would be alright. However, it was not alright! I felt like I was dying inside. My room had begun to feel like a prison. I was confined to it day and night.

When I walked into my room, my sister Mary asked what was wrong. I begin to tell her that I did not feel pretty, that I felt ugly

29

and unwanted. She looked at me and said, "I love you, and you are the most beautiful sister in the whole world." Then she gave me the biggest hug. This really touched my heart, because we didn't always get along. We would argue, fight and call each other names based on our skin complexion. She had a much darker skin complexion than mine, so I would call her an ugly black dog and she would call me an ugly half-white dog due to my lighter complexion. We would do this often, especially when we were mad at each other.

Chapter 6

Emotions Running High

Webster's dictionary defines emotion as a strong feeling (such as fear, wonder, love, sorrow, and shame) often accompanied by a physical reaction, blushing, trembling, or some other facial reaction. Your mind uses the information it receives to activate your emotions. If the information is positive, your emotions are positive, if negative, then they are negative.

My emotions have been all over the place. I have suffered abuse at the hands of family members. I have been threatened and called everything but a child of God by my friend's dad on a bus full of other students. I have witnessed domestic violence and abuse day after day in my home. I am not sure what to do or how to feel. Things have gotten so bad that I started pretending that I didn't exist. This was no way for a young girl to live, but it didn't seem like things were getting any better for me.

I remember my sister and I coming home from school one day to find a strange car in the driveway. We had no idea who it could be. As we walked into the house we saw a lady that we did not recognize. We politely said hello and went to our room. You see, when we were growing up, you did not stay in a room where adults were talking. However, that did not stop us from hiding around the corner to see if we could hear what was being said. Apparently, we had missed the majority of the conversation because not long after we got home the lady got up to leave. But before she left we heard her tell our mother to call her if she changed her mind. The lady was my dad's other woman, and she wanted my mother to walk away from their marriage and let her have my dad. This lady went so far as to offer to pay my mother child support and to make sure that we never wanted for anything. My mother told her that she would not be changing her mind and that she was not willing let her have her husband.

When the lady finally left, my dad emerged from his hiding place. He was hiding in the back of the house. My sister and I were shocked and surprised to see him. But we were also happy that he did not catch us listening to our mother and the lady talking.

My mother set the table and we sat down to eat. But before we could take the first bite, the argument started. My sister and I looked at each other across the table. We knew it was about to be a very long night. Just then our mother made us leave the table. She told us to make a sandwich and go to our room, which we did.

My emotions were all over the place. I wondered what direction the fight that was about to take place between my parents would go. Would we wake up the next morning and one of them was seriously hurt? What would happen to my sister and me if this lady got her wish? Everyday was not a bad day at home. There were good times too. Like when my dad came home and he was happy and sober. Or when my mom and dad actually got along.

Well, in case you are wondering, we woke up the next morning and both mom and dad were alright. We got dressed and went to school to finish out the school year. It was the beginning of summer break. I was not excited about summer break, because it meant missing my friends and chopping cotton. Chopping cotton was how we got the money to buy our school clothes for the next

33

school year. I hated it, because I was not very good at it. I would chop down the cotton along with the weeds. That was until one day my mother told me that it was going to start being deducted from my pay. I quickly learned to do it right after that! This went on every summer for years.

Finally one summer, I had the opportunity to meet the lady that was with my dad before my mom and was the mother of his other children. Her name was Ms. Olivia and she had several children both sons and daughters by my dad, and she brought them to see him. She seems to be a really nice lady and she always treated me with kindness. I was excited to meet my other siblings, especially my sister Faye, because she was beautiful and I could see the resemblance between she and I. Faye and I hit it off, and when they were about to leave Ms. Olivia invited me and my sister to come to their house in Memphis for a visit. Mary said no, because she didn't want to go anywhere unless my mother went also. I was happy to go so that I didn't have to keep chopping cotton.

Things went well the first few days of my visit. Faye and I were getting along like sisters; we even walked to see her boyfriend one day. When we returned home, our bother met us stating that he had been looking for us. He stated that Ms. Olivia had gotten sick and been admitted to the hospital. He was very angry with us and said that he was going to make us pay for the fact that he could not get in touch with us. Before I knew anything, he had taken out a belt and begin whooping my sister. I am not sure what else happened between the two because he took her into another room. Then he came after me. He took me into a room and threw me down on the bed and starting trying to take my clothes off. I was fighting and trying my best to hold on to my clothes until he pulled out a knife and threatened to kill me. I was terrified, how could this be happening to me and why is Faye allowing it? I thought she and I were close, how could she stand and watch him do this to me? I really believe he had raped her as well. Because when it was all over, she apologized to me and tried her best to console me.

He made us get cleaned up and get ready to go to the hospital to see Ms. Olivia. He told us that we better not say anything about what happened because it would kill Ms. Olivia and we would be the cause of it. How could he turn this around on us like this?

He was a master manipulator. Not long after the rape, he took me back home to my parents in Arkansas. When I made it home and tried to tell my parents what happened to me I found out that he had beat me to the punch and lied to my parents. He told them that he was bringing me home because I was in Memphis hanging out with boys. I just looked at him! I could not hide the disgust and sheer hatred that I now had for him. What made matters worst is that my parents believed his lies and even allowed him to come and live with us from time to time. He made my life a living hell! Just his very presence sent me on an emotional roller coaster. I was angry, sick and fearful, suicidal and even homicidal at times. His actions forever changed my life.

I was having a hard time processing my emotions. My life up until this point has been filled with so much hurt, pain, and abuse. I thought about committing suicide, but I knew that was wrong. I started lashing out at people who had nothing to do with my pain. I knew that was wrong as well. So I begin to pray that God would give me the courage and the strength to make the best decisions. I prayed that he would not allow me to give in to the negative emotions or react out of anger. It was then that I realized that God alone could fill the emptiness that I felt. I prayed and God gave me a sense of peace and comfort.

A few years went by, and the arguments between my parents were getting worst. I remember one argument in particular; we were all sitting down watching TV and my mom and dad begin to argue because my mom was spending a lot of time away from home. I had taken on a lot of the motherly duties, like cooking, cleaning and watching out for my siblings, my brother Richard was a baby at the time. I always tried to make sure that my dad had a meal when he came home from work. The argument between my parents seems to escalate quickly. My mother spoke to my dad in a way that we had never known her to. She caught all of us off guard especially my dad. My dad finally told her that she could just go back where she came from. My dad was sitting in the chair rocking my brother Richard. The next thing we knew my mom had come out of the kitchen with a large knife and hit my dad in the head. There was blood everywhere. I grabbed my brother Richard and my brother Johnny grabbed the knife from my mom. Johnny then went to check on my dad to see if he was still breathing. I was so emotional! My siblings were yelling, screaming and crying. Had the day that we all feared come? Had our mother killed our father?

The police and ambulance came and they made us go in another room while they checked on our dad. He was later taken to the hospital for treatment. The doctors told my dad that if the cut had gone any deeper, my dad would have died. Even after being told that my dad still refused to press charges against my mother. This incident caused me to see my dad in a different light. From that day on, he could do no wrong in my eyes. It changed my father as well, he begin to take us with him everywhere he went. One day he even took us to the home of the woman that came to our home that day trying to get my mother to let her have my dad.

She was an older lady, much older than my mother, but she was nice and treated us kindly. Her and my dad had a daughter together whom we met that day.

A little while after the incident, my parents decided to call it quits. My mom decided that we were going to move to Blytheville. I was upset, I did not want to leave my school, my friends or have to prove myself to a new group of teachers. Mary didn't care, as long as she was with our mother. Mom was going back and forth to Blytheville to try to get things settled, so we were left with our dad.

I was once again on an emotional roller coaster. Things were changing so much around me. My parents are getting a divorce or at least separating. We were being left at home alone a lot. My dad was trying to work and provide for us, but his late hours meant that we didn't always get the proper food and nourishment. I would often walk to my grandmother's house for food and comfort.

One day while walking back from my grandmother's house I ran into my dad and he started walking with me. He begins talking to me about my mother. He looked and sounded so sad; that I reached out to give him a hug and tell him that everything was going to be ok. There was something different about the way my dad hugged me. It was entirely too long and too tight. I felt so uncomfortable. While he was hugging me, he whispered in my ear and told me that he and my mother were no longer sleeping together. He was breathing heavily and he tried to touch me inappropriately. I was mortified! I pulled away from him and ran as fast as I could home.

I made it home and told my sister Mary that I was going to kill daddy if he came in our room. I went into the kitchen and got a knife and put it under my pillow. I wrote a letter to my mother telling her what had happened. After my mother read the letter she came to my room, took the knife I had under my pillow and whooped me for saying that I was going to kill my dad. I couldn't seem to catch a break.

I was now terrified of my dad. I was afraid to be in the same house with him, so as much as possible; I kept my distance from him. I stayed in my room as much as I could so I didn't have to look at him. This worked until one day my mom decided to return to Blytheville to make final arrangements for the move. She decided that she would leave us with our dad. I begged and pleaded for her not to leave me there with him. I told her that he was going to rape me if she left me there. She didn't seem to care! She told me that I was going to stay, and that if I did not get back in that house she would shoot me! I never saw this coming, even in my wildest dreams! My mother was actually threatening to shoot me! Not only did she threaten to do it, she actually came into the house, got the shotgun, pointed it at me and pulled the trigger! All I could see was the dirt around my feet moving as that shotgun shell hit it, only inches from my feet. I had to ask the Lord for forgiveness because before I knew it, I had called her a terrible name and said she is trying to kill me.

I was an emotional wreck! I went back to the house for fear of being killed. She followed me and made me apologize to my dad for the things that I said about him. When she left, my dad apologized to me, but he never told my mother that he had touched me inappropriately. This caused me to start acting out. My behavior became so reckless. I acted as if I didn't have a care in the world. I was only 13 years old, but it seemed as if I had already lived a lifetime of hurt, pain and abuse.

We finally moved to Blytheville. I started a new school and began to play basketball and run track again. It wasn't the same as it was at my old school, because here I had to compete for my starting spot on the basketball team. I had to prove that I deserved that spot every day. That didn't last long because within a year I was changing schools again. I didn't really like this school because I was the new girl again. I was the target of a lot of the boys at school; they were trying their best to get me in a sexual relationship with them.

Since I came into the school late that year, I ended up having to go to Summer School. Summer school was not as strict as regular school and I begin to become close friends with some of the boys.

I found myself becoming too trusting, and forgot what I had been told about the mindset of teenage boys. I had a crush on one of the boys whose name was Steven. He was very athletic; he was on the football team and could have any girl he wanted. As a matter of fact many of them were throwing themselves after him. However, I was shy and I acted like I was just one of the guys.

One day, one of my friend girls asked me to walk home with her so I did. As we were walking, I noticed that several of the boys were following us. We stopped at a burger joint that was on our way and they came in too. We ordered a couple of milkshakes and sat down at a table. All of a sudden she wanted to go to the bathroom, and wanted me to go with her. I told her that I would stay and watch our drinks, but she insisted that I go with her. Even though I was uncomfortable leaving our drinks with the boys, I gave in and went with her and we asked the boys to watch our drinks for us. When we came out, they gave us our drinks, but they gave her a look that I didn't understand at the time. For some reason, I felt uneasy about drinking the milkshake, but I drank it anyway.

A little while later as we were walking home I started to feel lightheaded and dizzy. My friend girl said that she would help me get home and into my house. She said maybe that milkshake made you sick. When we started walking the boy she liked told her he wanted her to go with him, and he said that Wayne could take me in the house. I begged her not to leave me, because I could only see shadows and I was really scared, but she did anyway.

I must have blacked out because all I remember is waking up with my mother standing over me asking me why I was sleeping in the middle of the day. She asked me what was wrong with my clothes. I was confused, because I didn't remember much after walking home. I got up to take a bath and that's when I realized that something sexual must have happened to me while I was blacked out. I went and told my mother, but she really didn't want to hear it. How do I keep finding myself in this position? Why am I never believed? Every time I think things are going well, I get taken for another ride on the emotional roller coaster.

44

Well about a month passes and I start feeling sick and throwing up everywhere. My mom and my aunt Addie took me to the doctor to see what was going on with me. The doctor asked to do a pap smear, which I did not feel I needed because I was a virgin. However, I couldn't be certain, because I didn't remember exactly what happen to me that day. Long story short, I was forced to take the Pap smear and the doctor told my mom that I was pregnant.

I thought my life was over! With all that I have been through how could I become a mother? My mom was furious! There was nothing that I could say to her to make her see my side of things. She called me everything she could think of except my name. Not only did she talk bad to me and about me, she told everyone that I was pregnant. My aunt Addie tried her best to explain to my mother that I had been the victim of a date rape, without success.

I can't even begin to tell you the emotional pain that I was experiencing at that time. I had been victimized, became pregnant and was then blamed for something that I had no control over. I just wanted to run away! I thought my prayers had been answered when my aunt and uncle in Texas agreed to let me come and stay with them, but there was a catch. I had to have an abortion! I couldn't imagine having an abortion after all that I have already been through. But how can I finish school and raise a baby at only 14 years old?

I decided that no matter what, I was going to keep the baby and try to finish school. However, shortly after becoming pregnant my mother started making me babysit my younger siblings, causing me to miss school. I felt hopeless. How would I ever fulfill my dream of becoming a doctor or a lawyer?

I was an emotional wreck as the time to deliver my baby drew near. I was afraid that the pain would be so bad that I would die. I was afraid of the possibility of losing my baby. How would I react being a teenage mother? Would I make the same mistakes that my mother made with me? Would I treat my children better and be there for them? Well I guess time would have to answer those questions for me because delivery day is here! I gave birth to a bouncing baby boy and I named him Bryan.

Not long after Bryan was born, I moved in with a nice older lady name Earnestine! She would keep Bryan for me so that I could go to school and finish my education. I was nervous about leaving him with her at first, but she took good care of him. Later, I started dating her son whose name was William. The relationship started out good, but before I knew it, he had become very abusive. We would fight every day. To make matters worst, his mother took up for him, saying that he was only trying to make me strong. I had no idea what she meant by that, because even though I had suffered a lot of abuse in my life, I didn't think it was right in any form. I didn't know everything, but I knew this wasn't right and I needed to break free!

This went on for about a year, until my mother found a place to live that was big enough for my son and I to move back in with her. Everything seemed to be going fine for a while. My mom has made friends with the neighbors and she spends a lot of time at their house. It wasn't long, before we found out that my mom was sleeping with the neighbor's husband. This led to all sorts of problems, and before long, I had fallen victim once again to the abuse of a man. My mother sent me to the store with a neighbor's husband and he took advantage of me. As a matter of fact, he raped me, but told my mother that I had taken off my clothes in his car. She believed him, without question.

After this incident, I gave up and begin self-destructing. I started drinking, smoking and having sex. I just didn't care. I was so broken, hurt and confused. I just wanted to get away from it all. I wanted something to numb the pain. I didn't want to feel anything. I put myself in some very dangerous positions and situations because I was running from my feelings. To be honest, I really don't know how I made it this far, other than to say it was the grace of God. He kept me through it all.

I promised myself after a few close calls with trouble that I would straighten up my act. That promise was short lived, although it was not because I had broken it. My mother had met a man at the club who came by looking for a good time. He asked my mom if he could have my sister Mary, but my mom refused saying she was too young. But she told him that she had another daughter that had just had a baby that he could have, which was me. This man took me to his house, pumped me full of alcohol and marijuana and took advantage of me. This was not a one-time occurrence; it went on for months, until I ended up pregnant again. I was devastated because of my recent behavior; I had no idea who the father could have been. Was it this man or one of the other guys I had been with? How was I going to make it being 16 years old with 2 kids and no fathers for either one of them? I was at my lowest, but I didn't believe in abortion, so I had the baby. Another son!

Chapter 7

God Has A Plan

I am now sixteen with 2 children. Things are still crazy at home so I move in with my aunt Anna. I started going to church with her and that is where I met the man I was going to later marry. I remember it like it was yesterday. We were in revival and Dewayne and his brothers were the gospel group that was singing that night. Their voices were so amazing! After they were done singing, they came to the back of the church where I was and sat down. We began talking back and forth.

While we were talking, the prophet that was speaking called for me to come to the front. I tried to pretend that I did not know that it was me that he was speaking to, but Dewayne's brother Jeremy looked at me and said, "he's talking to you." I finally look up and the prophet is pointing directly at me, saying yes you! I stood up and slowly walked to the front of the church where he was standing and he began to prophesy to me. He said, that I was called and chosen to do the will of God. He said every time God has something for you the devil throws a monkey wrench at you

50

to get you off course. This was hard for me to believe, especially the way that my life had been up until this point. I had no idea that my life was about to take another turn.

After church, I left with Dewayne and his brothers. Dewayne and I started talking, and he told me about all of the houses, cars, and money that he had. I guess he was trying to impress me, however, I was not impressed with those things. Especially since I later found out that he didn't have any of them. That didn't keep me from wanting to be with him. I thought he just might be a part of God's plan for my life. Dewayne ended up moving to St. Louis for a while to live with his brother. I was so distraught; I really felt that he was the man for me.

I was really missing Dewayne, so I decided to go the local club where my dad was shooting dice. When I got there, the owner of the club told me that I had to leave because I was underage, and he did not want the police to raid his club because of me. My dad told me to go home, and asked a young man that he knew to take me. I really didn't get a good vibe from the young man, but I went because my dad insisted.

When I got in the car with the young man, he stated that he had to make a stop somewhere on the way. He offered me something to drink, but I refused. The next thing I knew, we were on a dark gravel road in the country. I was afraid for my life, because I had no idea where I was. He begins to force me to drink the alcohol that he had with him. He also took out some marijuana and made me smoke blunt, after blunt. I couldn't believe that I was in a situation like this again! I complied with commands in hopes that I would survive the ordeal. I just wanted to make it home to see my babies. He begins to climb on top of me, and starts to rape me. I began freaking out! When I did he got up off me, and I took off running! I had no idea where I was or where I was going. I was seeing black dots, I couldn't catch my breath, and I was totally freaking out! He chased me down until he caught up with me and promised to take me straight home and not to try anything else. I later found out that he was afraid of going to jail if something had happened to me, because the marijuana he had given me had been laced with crack cocaine.

Once I made it home, I called my friend Michael over because I was afraid of what might happen to me. I told Michael what happened and he thought I might have been overdosed. So Michael came and spent the entire night with me. He kept walking me up and down the street in an attempt to keep me awake. Michael found a telephone number for Dewayne in St. Louis and calls to tell him what happened. Dewayne is upset and quickly returns to Arkansas to be with me.

Dewayne and I became an official couple. He said I was the only girl for him. I was so in love with him, and he seemed to love me too. Things between us were going well. I thought that my life was finally turning around for the better. Dewayne was a godly church going man, or so I thought! Shortly after becoming an official couple Dewayne started cheating with some of his old girlfriends. He started trying to separate me from my friends and family. Not long after that the abuse started, even though we were both active in the church.

I had to learn to pray a lot and to forgive a lot living my life with Dewayne. It wasn't all bad; we had some good times too. But sometimes, even our good times, turned bad. I remember one night, Dewayne took my sister and me to Beale Street in Memphis for a night out on the town. We had an amazing time; in fact, we had the time of our lives. That is until we were on the way home. My sister and I had fallen asleep. We were awaken by the sound of the truck crashing and flipping over. Gas was leaking everywhere and we were trapped in the truck. Dewayne must have been ejected from the truck, because he was nowhere to be found when the truck finally landed. A few people who witnessed the accident pulled us from the truck. As we lay side by side on the ground, we were very afraid. We held hands and told each other I love you, not knowing if we were going to make it. When we made it to the hospital my sister, who was 8 months pregnant, had been thrown from the back seat to the front, and had a broken arm and broken leg. My pelvic bone was broken.

Once at the hospital, my sister was taken into labor and delivery where she gave birth to my nephew Joseph. I was taken down to radiology to have an x-ray performed. When I got there the x-ray tech had me to stand and walk to the table for the x-ray. I was in so much pain.

Later when the doctor came in I was told that my bones shifted when I walked to the table and there was a possibility that I could end up paralyzed from the waist down. Not only that, the x-ray showed that I was pregnant. He said that I may need to abort this pregnancy and that there was a strong possibility that I would not be able to have any more children. I told the doctor that I would not be aborting my baby. The doctors and my mother were highly upset with me, because I refused to abort my child.

I prayed and talked to God about it and I was ready to leave the hospital. The doctor came in and I asked him if I could be discharged, he stated you are not ready. I told him that I would sign myself out. He told me that I couldn't because I was a minor. I asked my mother to sign me out and she refused. I really wanted to get out of there so I could go and see my sister. I finally

told the doctor that I was married and I was able to sign myself

out. My mother drove me home, but she refused to let me go and

see my sister before leaving the hospital.

The next day, while at home I received a phone call from the

hospital saying that they were trying to reach my mother. They

stated that something had gone wrong and they needed to do

emergency surgery on my sister. I finally located my mother and

told her what the doctors said, and that she needed to get to

Memphis to the Trauma Center. She did not leave right away. She

was running around trying to find her husband and see what he

was doing. When she finally left and headed to Memphis, the

hospital called and said that my sister had passed away from a

blood clot. I never imagined the night we spent on Beale Street

would be our last. Or when I told her that I loved her lying on the

street after the accident, that it would be our last time seeing each

other. My sister was only 14 years old at the time. I was

devastated! Why didn't my mother make it to the hospital in

time? Maybe if she had gone straight to the hospital instead of looking for her husband, my sister would not have died. I had to have someone to blame, so I blamed my mother.

Then I started to wonder, how could God allow this to happen? Why didn't he spare my sister's life? I had to keep telling myself that everything happens for a reason. That God does not make mistakes. That God has a purpose and a plan for everything that He allows to happen. As I was praying for peace and comfort, God reminded me that my sister had said so many times that she wanted to die and she was ready to go. As a matter of fact, the night before the accident, she told me that so much was going own at home that she wished she was dead. Although my heart was broken that she was gone, I had to believe that God had a plan and that she was in a better place.

Chapter 8

From Unforgiveness to Forgiveness

My life up unto this point has been filled with so much hurt, pain and disappointment. It seems as if every time I think that the struggles are over for me another problem arises. I have found myself hating everyone, my mother, father, abusers and even myself at times. It took me a long time to realize that until I could forgive myself and those that hurt me, I would continue to be miserable, and God knows I have endured enough misery!

You see, forgiveness is much easier said than done. Even when you know that forgiveness is for you and not them. I had bottled up so much pain, that I had become bitter, angry and unforgiving. It was taking a toll on my life. My blood pressure was high and I was experiencing issues with my heart. I had to make a decision, would I hold on to the bitterness and unforgiveness and let it kill me? Or would I let it go and live? I chose to let it go and live. My abusers have gone on with their lives. They are not even concerned about me. The pain was not worth holding on too. In fact, nothing that I had experience was worth dying for. God had spared my life and kept me around for a reason, and I was not going to let my abusers have another minute of my life.

When you decide to forgive, you can expect opposition from the devil. He does not want to you walk in the freedom that forgiveness gives. He wants to keep your mind and your heart in bondage. He wants you to inflict the pain you feel on those around you. He wants your bitterness to spread. This is what happens when you can't let go of the past. You make every person you encounter pay for what happened to you.

I've learned that when you forgive others, God will forgive you. Forgiveness opens the door for complete and total restoration. God wants to restore you, but how can He when you are so consumed with what has happened to you. You have to submit to the process and part of the process is forgiveness. Forgive your parents, your abusers, your spouse and anyone else that has wronged you.

I didn't know what it meant to be restored. I questioned why did I even need it? Then I realized that I had been broken and God wanted me to be made whole. I had been weak and God wanted me to be strong. I wasn't the best version of myself. I needed God to give me the strength to become better.

Because of the abuse that I had endured most of my life, I went through a period of self-hatred and self-destruction. I battled mental, physical, and spiritual strongholds. Some of them were forced upon me, and others of them I took upon myself. I had to ask God to forgive me for the things that I had done to myself, like the drinking, smoking and pre-marital sex. Then I asked God to break every generational curse that I was born under that was still causing pain in my life. I asked God to take away everything in me that was not like him. Like King David, I asked Him to create in me a clean heart and to renew a right spirit within me.

Forgiving those that hurt me was not easy, as a matter of fact it was one of the hardest things I have ever done. But at the same time it was one of the best things I have ever done for myself. I hope that by sharing my story with you, it will give you the strength that you need to forgive those that have wronged you. I pray that you can make peace with your past and embrace your future.

Life can break you down. But you don't have to be destroyed. I have been at my lowest, more times than I can count. But through it all God has never left me nor forsaken me. He has been a very present help in my times of trouble. He can put your life back together again. Give Him your brokenness and He will make you whole!

Remember the word of the Lord in Psalms 34:18 says, The Lord is nigh unto them that are of a broken heart; and saveth such as be of a contrite spirit. Psalms 147:3- He healeth the broken in heart, and bindeth up their wounds. God is ready, willing and able to forgive you and to heal you everywhere you hurt. His word declares in Psalms 103:3- Who forgiveth all thine iniquities; who healeth all thy diseases; All you have to do is cry out to Him! You can be made whole today! Psalms 34:6 -This poor man cried, and the Lord heard him, and saved him out of all his troubles.

www.ingramcontent.com/pod-product-compliance
Lightning Source LLC
Chambersburg PA
CBHW032034090426
42741CB00006B/813